A LOOK AT PHYSICAL SCIENCE

LIGHT AND COLOR

BY KATHLEEN CONNORS

 Gareth Stevens
PUBLISHING

CRASHCOURSE

Please visit our website, www.garethstevens.com. For a free color catalog of all our high-quality books, call toll free 1-800-542-2595 or fax 1-877-542-2596.

Cataloging-in-Publication Data

Names: Connors, Kathleen.
Title: Light and color / Kathleen Connors.
Description: New York : Gareth Stevens Publishing, 2019. | Series: A look at physical science | Includes index.
Identifiers: LCCN ISBN 9781538221532 (pbk.) | ISBN 9781538221518 (library bound) | ISBN 9781538221549 (6 pack)
Subjects: LCSH: Light--Juvenile literature. | Color--Juvenile literature.
Classification: LCC QC360.C645 2019 | DDC 535--dc23

First Edition

Published in 2019 by
Gareth Stevens Publishing
111 East 14th Street, Suite 349
New York, NY 10003

Copyright © 2019 Gareth Stevens Publishing

Designer: Samantha DeMartin
Editor: Kristen Nelson

Photo credits: Series art Creative Mood/Shutterstock.com; cover, p. 1 Pavel_Klimenko/Shutterstock.com; p. 5 (lamp) Lijphoto/Shutterstock.com; p. 5 (flame) MICROSONE/Shutterstock.com; p. 5 (flashlight) MargoLev/Shutterstock.com; p. 5 (christmas lights) FoapAB/Shutterstock.com; p. 7 oorka/Shutterstock.com; p. 9 Designua/Shutterstock.com; p. 11 Happy Stock Photo/Shutterstock.com; p. 13 ferocioussnork/Shutterstock.com; p. 15 Praphan Jampala/Shutterstock.com; p. 17 AHonaker/Shutterstock.com; p. 19 (transparent) wavebreakmedia/Shutterstock.com; p 19 (translucent) SOLOTU/Shutterstock.com; p. 19 (opaque) joloei/Shutterstock.com; p. 21 Ray B Stone/Shutterstock.com; p. 23 (both) GIPhotoStock/Science Source/Getty Images; p. 25 (top) Yana Alisovna/Shutterstock.com; p. 25 (bottom) mikeshinmaksim/Shutterstock.com; p. 27 Pressmaster/Shutterstock.com; p. 29 piyaphong/Shutterstock.com; p. 30 (rainbow) EGOR_21/Shutterstock.com; p. 30 (prism) Pro Symbols/Shutterstock.com; p. 30 (eye) browndogstudios/Shutterstock.com.

Printed in the United States of America

CPSIA compliance information: Batch #CS18GS: For further information contact Gareth Stevens, New York, New York at 1-800-542-2595.

CONTENTS

Words in the glossary appear in **bold** type the first time they are used in the text.

ALL THE LIGHT WE CAN SEE

The light from a lamp or flashlight is visible light, or the light people can see. There are also other kinds of light people can't see. All light is **electromagnetic** radiation. Radiation is **energy** that moves and spreads out as it moves.

MAKE THE GRADE

Visible light is one small part of the electromagnetic **spectrum**.

5

WHAT'S *LIGHT?*

Light is made up of tiny **particles** called photons. The movement of electrons creates photons. Sometimes, an electron gains energy and it moves to a higher place, or orbital, in an atom. When it falls back down, it gives off a photon.

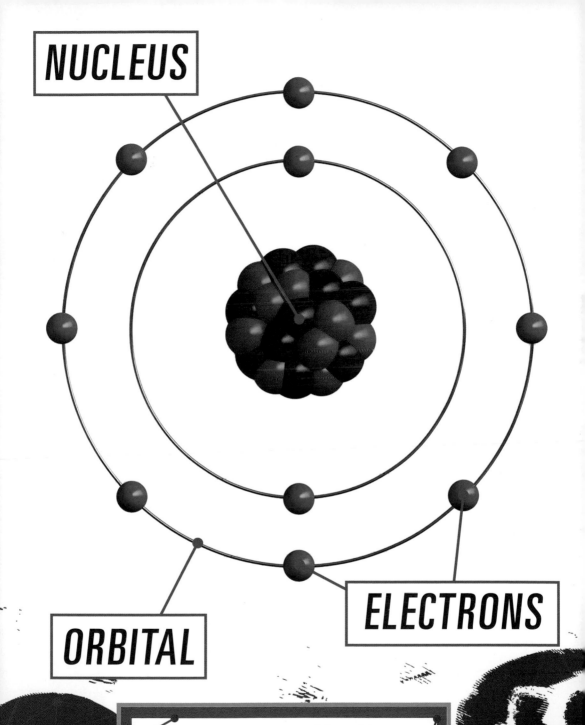

NUCLEUS

ELECTRONS

ORBITAL

MAKE THE GRADE

Electrons are the negatively charged
parts of an atom.

Light moves through space as a wave. A wave is something that travels through space and matter, moving energy from one place to another. Light, which is part of the electromagnetic spectrum, can have short or long wavelengths.

MAKE THE GRADE

Gamma rays have the shortest wavelengths on the electromagnetic spectrum. Radio waves have the longest. Visible light is in the middle of the spectrum.

THE
ELECTROMAGNETIC
SPECTRUM

10^3

RADIO
WAVES

1

MICROWAVES

10^{-3}

INFRARED
RADIATION

10^{-5}

VISIBLE
LIGHT

10^{-7}

ULTRAVIOLET
LIGHT

10^{-9}

X-RAYS

10^{-11}

10^{-13}

GAMMA RAYS

9

HEAT MAKES LIGHT

To create photons, atoms need energy. Atoms are often energized by heat. For example, in older light bulbs, electricity causes the **filament** inside to get so hot it gives off light. Combustion, or burning, is another way photons are created.

MAKE THE GRADE

Combustion occurs when matter mixes with the gas oxygen and gives off heat and light.

11

FREQUENCY IS COLOR

The number of waves that move past a point in 1 second is the frequency of the wave. In visible light, frequency is called color. Photons have a color based on the energy given off by the movement of the electrons.

MAKE THE GRADE

Light with a high frequency also has high energy. Like the colors of the rainbow, "ROY G BIV" can help you remember the lowest energy color, red, and the highest, violet.

13

GOT WHITE?

Often, light, such as sunlight or the light from a lamp, looks like it doesn't have a color. It's often called "white" light. But that's not a color on the electromagnetic spectrum! White light is a mix of many colors.

MAKE THE GRADE

When metal starts to get hot, it glows red,
the lowest energy color. If heated more,
it glows white. That means lots of energy
has been added, and it's very hot!

REFLECTION

Light **interacts** with matter. When light hits a **surface** that's smooth, the light is given back. This is reflection. Light reflects off a smooth surface at an **angle** equal to the angle at which the light hits the surface.

MAKE THE GRADE

Light reflects off surfaces that aren't smooth, too. When light hits an uneven surface, it scatters, or reflects at all different angles. That's what lets us see what's on the surface!

16

17

PASSING THROUGH

Light cannot pass through some matter. This matter is called opaque. Wood and rubber are examples of opaque matter. Transparent matter, such as glass, allows visible light to pass through. Something on either side of the matter can be seen from the other side.

OPAQUE

TRANSPARENT

TRANSLUCENT

MAKE THE GRADE

Light can pass through translucent matter, but something on one side of the matter cannot be seen clearly through it.

REFRACTION

Both air and water are transparent **mediums**. When light waves move from one transparent medium to another, they change speed and bend. This is called refraction. How much the light bends depends on how much the waves slow.

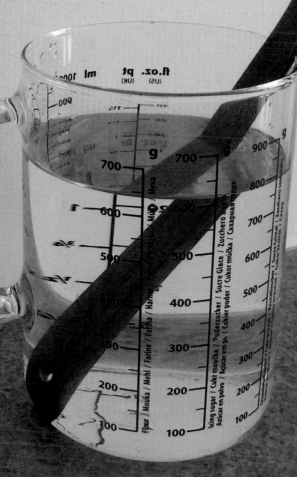

Lenses, such as those in a pair of glasses, use refraction. Lenses are made of transparent matter with curved sides. A convex lens is thicker in the middle. It bends light to **focus** on a certain point.

MAKE THE GRADE

A concave lens is thinner in the middle. It spreads out light rays.

CONCAVE

CONVEX

Scientists found a way to use refraction to separate white light into a rainbow of colors. By shining light through a prism, the different wavelengths are bent at different angles. This causes the colors to appear separately!

MAKE THE GRADE

A triangular prism is a solid, transparent object that has two triangular bases and three flat sides.

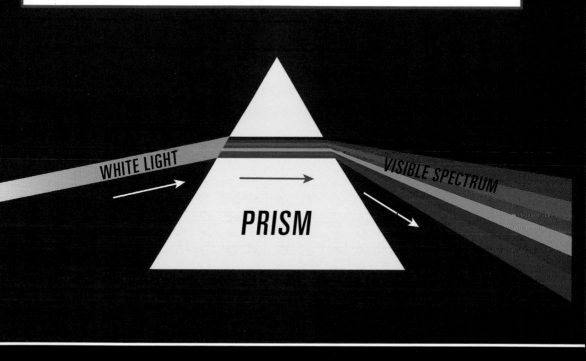

WHITE LIGHT

VISIBLE SPECTRUM

PRISM

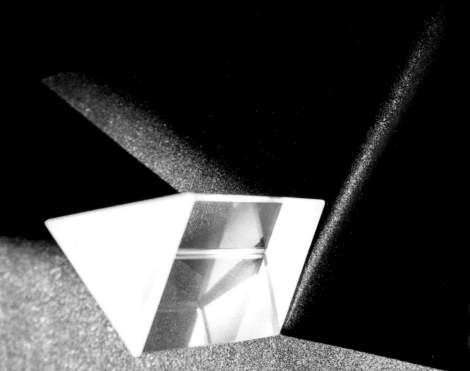

25

SEEING IN COLOR

Most objects around us have a color. That's because the matter they're made of and the paint or dye on them absorb, or take in, all the colors except the ones you see. The object reflects back the color, or frequency, that you see!

MAKE THE GRADE

Matter that looks white is reflecting all light's wavelengths. Something black is absorbing them all!

In order to see color, our eyes and brain work together. Parts of the eye called rods and cones receive light and pass it through the nerves to the brain. The brain then tells us what color we see!

MAKE THE GRADE

Many animals can see color, too. Some, such as bees, can see other kinds of light people can't see!

29

LIGHT AND COLOR
BASICS

 People can only see part of all the light around us.

Light is made up of particles called photons.

Light moves as electromagnetic waves.

Different colors have different wavelengths.

White light is a mix of all the colors.

Matter may reflect, refract, or absorb light.

 Color is seen because of the frequencies matter absorbs and reflects.

GLOSSARY

angle: the space that forms when two lines or surfaces come together at a point

electromagnetic: having to do with the relationship between electric currents and magnetism

energy: power used to do work

filament: a single thread or a thin, threadlike object inside older light bulbs

focus: to cause something to be directed at something else

interact: to have an effect on each other

medium: the matter or surroundings in which something happens

particle: a very small piece of something

spectrum: a range of something, such as light waves

surface: the top amount of something

vacuum: an empty space without any matter in it

FOR MORE INFORMATION

BOOKS

Bell, Samantha. *Color and Wavelengths*. Ann Arbor, MI: Cherry Lake Publishing, 2018.

James, Emily. *The Simple Science of Light*. North Mankato, MN: Capstone Press, 2018.

WEBSITE

Color—What Is Color?

www.crayola.com/for-educators/resources-landing/articles/color-what-is-color.aspx

Read more about color and find experiments and activities using what you've learned.

INDEX